Introduction to
UnBrokable*

5 Reasons
Why *People Go* **Broke**
Despite Working Hard

Brad Kong

*"**UnBrokable**** may be a word we cannot find in a dictionary yet, as I coined it: **A person who cannot be broke, financially."**

— Prologue in *UnBrokable*

Disclaimer

These are the full title and subtitle of this book:

Introduction to ***UnBrokable*:*** **Two** out of 80 **Reasons Why Being Broke Despite Working Hard**

   I wrote only "***Two Reasons Why Broke* Despite Working Hard**" on the front cover *intentionally* for rhyme, simplicity and focus.

The graphic on this book cover is from Edit.org. I use the site to design my covers; it provides book cover templates with its copy-righted images to writers who paid "annual memberships." I do have three proofs of my membership to Edit.org, payment receipt for the membership through Paypal and reference address to the image of the site. I am writing this because I received emails regarding my "book cover images" twice; both of which were resolved within a day. I decided to stick to my own or edit.org's images since I cannot keep getting copyright emails. If you have any issue regarding my cover art, feel free to contact me: I will be more than happy to provide the three proofs again.

Also by Brad Kong

Condo Chronicle
How to Lose 40 Pounds

Brad Short Story Collection II:

15 Things You Didn't Know About Korea
3 Reasons Why We Need to Buy a Home Early
Why Are CDs Super Important?
Say No To TSLA (2nd Edition)
Large Pizza for $5
30 Reasons Why I am Great
3 Reasons Why the Nursing Home Filed Bankruptcy
3 Mistakes Offline Small Business Owners Make
3 Lessons I have Learned from the Stock Market
My Friend Soo-young

Brad Short Story Collection III:

Why Are Orcas Friendly to Humans?

Quotist:

Quotist I
Quotist II
Quotist III

Praise for *UnBrokable*

"This is the best book I have ever read. I am saying this only because Brad is my husband."

-Tsina D,
A housewife and teacher

"I cannot believe my dad wrote this much thick book. He must be a genius."

-Yuna K,
An elementary school student

"I am proud of my son who wrote a book in English."

-Ms. Jin,
A wealthy woman

"Publishing this book is a celebration itself. Write your name on the next page if you bought this for a gift."

-Brad K,
A philosopher, writer, publisher, book designer and investor

Un*Brokable**

Dear _____

This book is my gift for you.
It has been helpful for me, so I hope it will be helpful
for you as well.
Thank you always.
Sincerely,

From _____

For all the hard *Workers*
Struggling Everyday

Contents

Prologue

Dying poor is a shame, especially in wealthy countries.
It is not about money – it shows how we have lived.
-Brad Kong

This is me sitting on the Ferrari in Miami, FL in 2003 – spending parents' money crazily. Then, I didn't expect I would go abysmally broke and suffer for a long time.

Hamas from Palestine invaded Israel in October 2023. A war broke out instantly and over 50,000 people have died so far. I am not talking about anti-Zionism, but if I were Israelis, I wouldn't have tried to expand my territory against Palestinians. Technically, **the land of current Israel doesn't have much commercial values – no oil, agriculture or water resources.** I would try to keep some lands over Tel Aviv, which is more than 10 times bigger than Hong Kong or Singapore, and try to build a city like Dubai. I wouldn't have fought over useless lands with poor Palestinians; I would rather let them keep most of it, as I need what I need. **The fact that we don't think practically can be a reason to be poor.** *Land used to have "absolute values"* in agricultural societies, an *old concept*, not applicable any more. Also, I wouldn't stick to Jerusalem itself, only because my ancestors used to live there. The *point* is to obtain new land for Jewishs to settle safely. 90% of Australia or Canada are virtually empty. I wonder what would Moses do if he governs now – by the time he led the Exodus[1] out of Egypt, North America was not even discovered yet.

Jack Whittaker was a construction businessman in Putnam County, WV – the winner of a lottery jackpot of $315 million in 2002. He was a millionaire already with a net worth of $17 M before winning – a rich man who won a bonanza. However, oddly a series of unfortunate events happened to him afterwards. First, a guy named Tribble, the boyfriend of Whittaker's granddaughter Brandi, was found dead from drug overdose in Whittaker's home in 2004; three months later, Brandi herself was also found dead at the age of 17; cocaine and methadone were found in her body. Five years later, Bragg (42), who was Whittaker's daughter and the mother of Brandi, was also found dead in Daniels, WV. Then, Whittaker's home in Bland County, VA, was reported to be on fire in 2016. Finally, Whittaker himself passed away following a long illness at 72 in 2020: *Why did the luckiest guy in the world pass away early, after losing all his children?* I turned 52 this year and the best thing I am glad about myself is that I haven't drunk or smoked for life; I am glad that I didn't

---

[1] 1,400 B.C.

damage my organs more than now, though my kidneys and teeth are somewhat impaired by drinking sodas for decades.

Han Liu was a Chinese billionaire, the former chairman of Hanlong Group known for mining businesses. His net worth was claimed at $6 billion USD by the time he passed away at 49 in 2015. He was convicted of murdering 8 people and running a mafia-style gang for businesses; he was executed by the law enforcement in China. His last words had been viral: "Life is short; *we don't have to live too tenaciously for more money*. I will have a small store next life and live happily with my family."

Those episodes gave me inspiration that we don't have to work to death, make a lot, spend and leave a fortune to others; I do not want to *grind* myself to donate more. In *Psychology of money* by Housel, there is a story of a man named Read – a janitor for 42 years, made a fortune out of blue-chip stocks, left $8 million to a hospital and passed away. I know a similar case of Groner – a secretary for 43 years, made profit out of the Abbott shares, left $7 million to a college and died. They were honorable. But, seriously, *what's the point?* What would be the thing they regretted the most? As long as I have enough, I conclude that **the best reward I can give to myself is *working less*.** I may not need a luxury car, but I like to save myself from drudgeries.

Have you ever been a dishwasher before? **If you don't fully agree with this book, it's possible you might not have been broke enough.** I believe a way to be *sufficient* is staying away from the reasons causing poverty. Coincidentally, I was in Chinatown Chicago the other day; it had some Korean shops, which were crowded. It took forever for Korea to be wealthy, but ironically, once its people became rich, they made money out of the condition: *Being prosperous can be a source of income itself.*

I bought my home in November, 2013. I didn't know it was the lowest price in the 21st century (source from Zillow).

I had $80,000 CDs in the bank in 2013: How do I recall it? I bought my condo for $60,000 that year; my real estate agent asked me to submit proof of funds in advance; I didn't know what to do, so I got a receipt from the ATM and gave it to her. Now I have over a $470,000 portfolio, not including my residence, as of 2025. This six times growth has probably been from investment success, salaries and frugality. But I would say that "not having rent or mortgages" played the most crucial role.

I see more "home sales signs" lately and recession may be looming in 2025. This book may not be for the super-rich, the middle-class or even mildly poor. I was in deep destitution, especially around 2009. My business wasn't doing well, after the subprime mortgage crisis broke out; my car was a decade old and horrible mechanics kept overcharging me; then my daughter was born in 2010. I couldn't waste even a cent for years, but I was able to manage to buy a small condo, thanks to my parents; the only advantage was all the housing prices collapsed due to foreclosures, caused by the heavy recession. This book is written for **unlucky people who have no idea how to get out of poverty.** The Ferrari photo upfront was taken 22 years ago – I had no idea how much trouble I was about to go through, then. Now I know being wealthy is a combination of survival skills, knowledge and *luck*. On the contrary, being broke can happen to anyone any time.

* * *

Charles Bukowski (1920 – 1994) was an American poet considered "the laureate of low-life" in the 1970s, who bought his first house 23 years *slower* than me. His net worth was over $4 million by the time he passed away: How did it happen? Bukowski was often considered a drunk loser, but I found he and I share a few things in common. First, we both started writing after our 40s; both had or have only one daughter. Both had worked for low income physical jobs; both inherited some money from parents after becoming middle-aged. Also, both were born in foreign countries, originally. But it shows *"Buk"* bought his first house with a mortgage at 58 (1979); I bought my condo in full at 40 (2013). It took an extra 5 years for him to pay off his

14

mortgage, so he ended up getting home title 23 years later than me: What made him take so long?

UnBrokable* may be a word we cannot find in a dictionary yet as I coined it: **A person who cannot be broke, financially** – the opposite of *Les Miserable*. Some live poor despite working full-time. More ironically, some live wealthy without having a job: *How? UnBrokable** series will be a practical, but unorthodox guide to stay away from *brokeness* – including unique reasons, examples and facts. **Brokeness** (not brokenness[2]) is a noun meaning **"the characteristic of not having enough money."** Have you ever been broke, despite having a job? Have you been short in spite of working full-time? People don't get broke automatically, especially in wealthy countries; if some are poor despite working, I believe there are reasons. *What does makes a person poor?* Why do some still rent an apartment after working 12 hours a day for 30 years? I had witnessed a couple of those closely for 7 years. I think there is a big misconception in our lives: If we work hard, we will be rich. Nothing can be further from the truth; *in fact, working longer can make us poorer;* some live painfully by exploiting themselves. I am a middle-aged man with a wife and daughter in the Midwest and my American life can be divided into four periods since 1999.

1. Colleges: Cornell and SUNY at Buffalo (1999-2005)
2. Business: Cyb Knight Video Games (2006-2014)
3. Employment: A nursing home (2015-2022)
4. Investor and writer (2022 - current)

Or I can divide the 26 years by jobs:

---

[2] *Broke**nn**ess* means "a condition in which something is badly damaged."

- College banquet (2001 - 2002)
- eBay seller (2003 - 2015)
- Cyb Knight Owner (2006-2014)
- Nursing home dishwasher (2015-2022)
- Investor and writer (2011-current)

There are other jobs with licenses (pharmacy technician and medical coder). Also I have worked as myriads of part timers since high school: convenience store clerk, bar kitchen helper, military soldier, etc.

* * *

Out of all those jobs, the recent *dishwasher* gave me the inspiration to write *UnBrokable** series. The nursing home I worked at is within walking distance from my home. I had a chance to volunteer to work there one day in 2015, unexpectedly, which brought me a permanent weekend position. Then, I had not done anything for a year after closing out my video game store for good in 2014. At the end of the work, they *wondered* if I could do the job at least every weekend. Now I see the reason why as I asked the questions to others myself; nursing homes always need employees while no one is excited to work there. Since they suggested a reasonable pay and plenty of free food from the kitchens, I accepted the offer. I had the job *only on weekends* for six years and on Sunday for a year, close to seven years in total.

I never liked that job since it was physically hard, but it had been helpful. First, I had chances to meet a lot of people I wouldn't without it – types of people doing dishwashing for life. Nothing wrong, but I think I was able to see reasons why they got stuck – **reasons for keeping them in chains.** Some were *truly great* guys, though. Secondly, the job had brought me physical strength and weight loss, especially in the beginning. Thirdly, these weekend extra salaries, bonus and free food still helped me build up my savings faster. There could be millions of reasons why people go broke: gambling, addictions, accidents, etc. **Nonetheless, there are others apparently not doing anything wrong, but always being broke**; many have nothing left after some payments withdrawal every month.

* * *

Do you know when I had the hardest time with money? While I worked at the video game store, my daughter was born in 2010. When a baby is born, parents need more money while physically exhausted. Incidentally, the mortgage bubble burst (2008) and severe depression came from 2009 (I guess businesses must have had a hard time during COVID era, too). While I had wasted my parents' money only to keep my store open, the only good thing I did was buying a condo in full. Since the economy collapsed in 2008, there had been plenty of foreclosures, short sales and discounted houses on the market – getting rid of my rent and mortgage for good was upside during that period.

After having difficulty with money myself and watching others struggle, I started wondering what really puts laborers in trouble – **Any *trap* to make full-timers broke, even in wealthy countries?** In the nursing home, I saw two dishwashers still renting apartments even after 30 years. They occasionally worked *double*, meaning up to 15 hours a day: Where did all their money go? Now, are you ready to jump into 80 chapters with examples? All the episodes are from my life or true events throughout history. By the time we reach the epilogue, I hope that we can be more mature, knowledgeable and close to wealth.

1

Drinking and Smoking

*All the poverties in the world originate
from drinking and smoking.*
- Brad Kong

Alexander the Great (356 – 323 BC) was an emperor of the
Greek kingdom of Macedonia, who had created the largest
empires in European history; his territory stretched from
Egypt to northern India, then. He was known to be
undefeated in battles and considered the greatest military
commander. While he had lived an extremely successful
life in general, his sudden downfall seemed to come with his
heavy drinking. The ruler impulsively killed "Cleitus the
Black," who saved Alexander's life once at a battle, during a
violent drunken altercation; it shows that Cleitus accused
him of judgmental mistakes that night. The monarch
deeply regretted the accident, but his severe alcoholism
likely started from that point. Alexander swam one day and
developed a mild fever possibly due to malaria; he spent
more days only on drinking and passed away – he was
32-years-old.

Yoon is the 13th president of South Korea elected in
2022. He was a prosecutor general previously, but I found
that he has an interesting record on Wikipedia; he had

failed his bar exams 9 times straight; in other words, it took 10 years for him to pass the legal test after college. We all know that passing a bar exam is not easy. Still, I believe most law students in college pass it after failing a couple times in Korea (Kim Kardashian passed it after failing three times while taking care of four kids). Coincidentally, this president is known for his *chronic alcoholism*; some believe that his numerous failures were due to his heavy drinking habit, which started when he was in college.

James Cook was a British explorer and the captain of the Royal Navy in the 18th century. He has been best known for his three voyages to New Zealand and Australia across the Pacific Ocean – finding sea routes never known before and discovering unknown islands as the first European. He also visited Hawaii as the first westerner in 1778. When the navy returned to Hawaii the next year, it shows that the military had a surprising welcome reception from the natives. Incidentally, it was a Hawaiian festival period to worship their Polynesian god Lono and they mistakenly believed that James was the deity who returned; the British decided to stay on the island for a month. Soon after, it turned out that the captain and crews had been drunk all the time, demanded too much alcohol, had fist fights with natives and harassed island women – as a result, the anger of the Hawaiians had grown.

One day, both parties had an exceptionally big quarrel over stuff stolen by Hawaiians from the English boats; the captain Cook tried to capture the King of Hawaii, "Kalani'ōpu'u" as a hostage to get their items back, but failed. Regretfully, the captain was stabbed to death at the age of 50 during the incident in 1779; four other marines were killed as well.

Did you know that it takes a lot of harvests to make a little amount of alcohol? That is why the Korean Joseon dynasty had occasional *prohibition eras*, whenever famines came. In a sense, making alcohol can be a global waste; drinking can promote our society to waste more grains and fruits. I believe that money drain starts from drinking, smoking or frequently both – these two seem to be the *most prevalent and common*. **I think that it is important to stop draining money first before trying to figure out how to make more.**

* * *

Amy Winehouse was an English singer and songwriter. She was 27 when she died of her noted alcoholism in London, England in 2011 – her net worth was about $4 M at the time of her death. Verne Troyer was an American actor and comedian – best known for his role of "Mini-Me" in the *Austin Powers* series. He died at 49 in Los Angeles, CA in 2018; his death was later ruled an alcohol poisoning; he was just about to get noticed after a long obscurity in his career. I have always thought that drinking and smoking are the biggest wastes, including *time*: 'I have wasted decades of my life, but I have never done it on drinking, at least.' It can cost our lives, too.

The *weekend* dishwashing job I had was like a Siberian death camp over the winter. I finished my army service by 1997, and still I don't see anything else I can compare it with. Countless people quit it within a week and I heard that a few even quit within 30 minutes. I truly wondered how some were able to keep it as full-timers for decades in that huge nursing home. There were *a couple of old Mexicans* who were unpleasant yet diligent. Quite frankly, the amount of wages, tips and bonuses I had received there was more than I expected. Besides, they gave me plenty of free food from the five restaurants inside it, continuously; I recall that I didn't have to go to supermarkets for months at a point. Since most people spend a good portion of their salaries on food, the job was actually a deal. I assumed it was how those Latinos were able to support their five children only by dishwashing – along with more benefits as full-time workers, too. **Regardless, the two were still renting apartments at the age of 60: *Why?*** There is an excerpt from the *Talmud*: A Jewish student asked, "Why are our pupils dark in the eyes?" A rabbi answered that, "It is better for us to see the dark side of life first."

* * *

Sadly, three ladies committed suicide together in Seoul, Korea in 2014: one mother and two daughters – not a common tragedy considering all the victims were grown-ups. Apparently, they burned coal in their small room, causing carbon monoxide poisoning. It showed that the mother was a 60-years old *eatery worker* and got laid off a month before this suicide pact. The two daughters were in their 30s; the elder one was unemployed due to diabetes; the younger one had a part time job at a graphic novel publisher, but had suffered from small wage, debt and bad credit. This demise had shocked the nation for a month, then. No one understood why this family could not get any support from the government. Eventually, the police concluded that the reason was financial hardship. Investigators and reporters checked the house thoroughly and found one grocery check book by the mother in the end. Not everyone writes all the spending thoroughly like her, so I could see that she had been honest and punctual.

(image from a Korean News)

Nonetheless, I couldn't help that a few items in their lists grabbed my attention: soju ($4.40), cigarettes ($20) and beers ($1.90 and $1.95). I thought that they passed away solely due to lack of money. I had been desperate myself, but in my case, I couldn't waste a single cent for a few years. Soju is a cheap but popular alcoholic drink in Korea – merely a diluted ethanol with sweetener (a small bottle is $10 from Amazon in 2022). Different from wine or beer, it does not have any taste at all except chemical – I actually saw that some Americans complained that it tastes just like

23

ethanol from a chemistry lab. I believe it was invented when the country was a ruin after the Korean war in the 1950s; I also assume that the country did not have much harvest to make a drink properly. Unexplainably, it is still one of Koreans' favorite drinks among the poor.

Nevertheless, I suddenly felt different as soon as I saw these in their purchases: "Why did they waste on alcohol and cigarettes, even when they were killing desperate?" I almost felt like they called for the consequence. Then, this hitted me: **Were drinking and smoking the reason making them broke from the start?** After all, soju is not a food we need to survive: in fact, it's not even a drink – merely a chemical, consisting of ethanol and sweetener. I don't have all the answers, but here is one thing for sure: they could have saved "that $28.25" in their pocket in 2014; little things change our lives from hell to heaven in destitute. More importantly, alcohol is known to cause depression which can lead to suicides.

* * *

I watched a documentary about Angel Falls in Venezuela the other day – heavy rainfall drops on top of the fall mountain everyday, which is the reason why the tops are flat by rain beats. Then, it shows that water comes down through the falls, goes to streams, rivers and all the way to the oceans. Then, **I thought that drinking and smoking are similar to those rainfalls;** these two habits may create minor problems in the beginning (e.g. wasting $10 bucks), but can continue all the way to oceans of bigger problems (e.g. liver failure).

Another analogy can be the human population. If all the problems are the eight billion human population now, drinking and smoking could be a couple of *Australopithecus* 4 million years ago. Some may think they are still wealthy despite those, but for sure, they could have been wealthier without them. When I was in college in Korea, I lived in a home-stay in 1992. I still remember that the brother of the landlady complained that he lost $2,000 cash, while he was drinking somewhere the other night. *I thought that losing that much was unbearable for me* (still is).

When I watched YouTube the other night, a popular Korean lady said all the expensive alcohols come out of our body as *urine* after all. I also watched a documentary about a fallen celebrity in Korea; there is the man who used to be a top singer 20 years ago, who was poor in 2023. It shows that he still wears a $10,000 coat and drinks $200 beers. One lady commented that, "The expensive clothes will stay, but pricey beers will go away." Alcohol is beyond *useless* damaging organs, but the truth is that virtually all types of drinks[3] except water is bad for our teeth – as a result, water is the only liquid I put in my mouth personally.

* * *

The last dynasty in the Korean peninsula was the Joseon (1392–1897). It had had several *Prohibition eras* officially recorded and **the penalty for the violation was death** – cutting heads by a machete in the 16th century. The record says that an official named Yune was also decapitated. Then, this was the king's reason for the strict prohibitions: "People are starved to death as there is no

---

[3] For example, soda, juice, coffee, etc.

grain left during famine. No one can eat a bag of rice, all at once. **Yet people can drink up a jar of alcohol overnight, made out of a bag of rice.**" It takes so much rice to make a small amount of alcohol, which can be consumed too quickly.

The issues of drinking and smoking often start with draining cash. Then, the damage continues on with things like getting headache, getting fined for DUI, fighting, losing teeth, getting concussion, having kidney malfunctions, etc. There is a Chinese foot massage place near my home – a middle aged couple owns it. I used to feel sorry for them since massaging feet for hours must be boring; I do not believe they charge a lot, either. I saw them closing their business door one night; they went straight to the liquor store across the street. Oddly, my sympathy diminished: 'Well, do they have money for that?' I thought. **While I owned my video game store, I didn't have a cent to waste,** as I had lost a little bit every month all the way throughout the eight years of the business ownership.

I do not believe that the couple ever understood that drinking could be the reason they got stuck there. I have never tried the place since it always looked deteriorating. I am not comfortable that some masseuses can have boring time because of me; simultaneously, window decals of the business were wearing off; I felt the business sinking with their habits. According to my observations, when owners don't drink and smoke, their store looks fresher even from outside; I know what my shop looked like.

* * *

I was a freshman in high school in Korea in 1989. At that time, the college entrance exam for highschoolers was exceedingly competitive and getting private tutoring from college students was popular. Korea was poorer and tutorings were not very expensive, then; a lot of college students did it for their part time jobs. One day, my mother brought a college student for my after-school tutoring. When I think about it now, she was not very wise; as a result, I ended up getting only lessons the whole day, instead of studying things on my own; she is not the type of person who decides things on her own; she always does what others do, blindly, which I hate. Anyway, the guy was attending mechanical engineering in Seoul National, the most prestigious in Korea (like Harvard in America). Unfortunately, his lessons were awful and not helpful for my grades at all. Above all, he had a violent unpleasant character, meaning he was not a teacher material, to begin with.

However, my parents were greedy and thought it was the best way for my brother and me. I felt like the parents thought my brother and I were the future income for them: he and I should get better grades and jobs, so we can support them with stable incomes later on. Anyway, that guy was from Busan where is far from Seoul. Eventually, except me, all of our family *agreed* that he should stay in our house for his own college study and our tutoring.

When I think about it now, that guy was nothing but a garbage. Even though he was only 22, he smoked crazily. One day, my smoker father visited his room and was shocked by how much cigarette odor was stuck in that room; that guy was a drinker, too. Since our home was far from his college even in Seoul, I recall that he skipped his classes a lot; later, the guy complained that he got five F's during a semester since he made a lot of effort to teach us, which is bullshit. Simply, he was a terrible college student not doing his job - **he failed because of him.**

What shocked me later was that his parents in Busan turned out to be extremely wealthy. My mother's hometown is also Busan, so I had a chance to visit his home, while I visited my grandma. I was surprised at the size of the house. I still remember he once smugly complained that his parents got $8 M USD fine from the IRS after an audit one year; it was believable considering the house. But, as a result of his poor grades, I learned that he could not study abroad in America, despite his parents' fortune. Korea is wealthier now, but still is a small and monotonous country. A lot of people are eager to get out of there for numerous reasons. In his case, I believe his seriously bad grades were the reason to block him from getting better opportunities.

When I checked him online in 2016, he seemed to own an English kindergarten in Korea – *a shame.* I guess the only job experience he had was tutoring, so he might have decided to go for it. I found out that his mother was a pharmacist[4] when I was at his house; seemingly, both of his parents studied well; I never liked that guy since he was physically violent to us. After all, he was a loser who wasted youth on heavy smoking.

---

[4] Not pharmacy technician

The reason why drinking and smoking are horrible is for their long term effects, including health issues; as a result, we can end up spending way more during our lifetime. Even for the super rich, our bodies are the most important assets. Considering an asset is something that brings money to us, does it make sense that a bar owner damages his own place and complains about lack of customers? I believe wealth building starts with protecting our most fundamental assets: Bodies. As Emerson said, "the first *wealth* may be *health*."

* * *

Summary

1. If you are serious about getting out of poverty, quit drinking and smoking first.
2. These two can connect us to millions of other headaches.
3. These two consume time, too.

2

Having too Many Children

Human population does not have to be bigger than it is
now.
-Brad Kong

Charles Dickens (1812-1870) was an English author who
wrote *Oliver Twist* and *A Christmas Carol*. He and his wife
Catherine married in 1836, when Charles was 24 and she
was 21. From then until the time of their divorce 22 years
later, *Catherine gave birth to 10 children.* It shows that
Dickens' own childhood had been bitter. At the age of 12,
with his father imprisoned for debt, he had to work in a
shoe factory, pasting labels on jars of shoe polish for a few
shillings each week – by then, his parents had eight
children and Charles was the second.

  Although I don't personally expect my daughter would be
a good money maker, which is perfectly fine, it seems
Dickens had thought differently. Unhappily, none of his
children turned out to be a successful writer like him and it
says he publically lamented that, "having brought up the
largest family ever known with the smallest talents to do
anything for themselves." In other words, he had to
virtually pay everything for his children until he passed
away. It shows that Dickens grew miserable about his
breeding eventually: The history recorded that **he**
resented the fact that he had so many children to

support. And, ironically, somehow, he saw it as his wife's fault. He didn't approve of Catherine's lack of energy, and began to indicate that she had never been his intellectual equal. In June 1858, Charles and Catherine filed for divorce, which was a little rare then, and he started seeing a new woman named Turnan.

I have only one child partly because I had a hard time, financially: Isn't it logical, though? No money, so I decided not to have more than I could afford. Unfortunately, to me, a lot of people, especially poor ones, don't seem to think this way; some give so many births no matter what. And I feel some fortify their poverty status that way: **It almost looks like that they make sure to be broke for the rest of their lives.**

* * *

Regrettably, Jennifer and Sarah Hart couple murdered their *six* adopted children by driving the family's SUV off a cliff in Mendocino County, CA in 2018; all eight people were in the vehicle during the accident. Police found the bodies of seven people in or near the crashed vehicle; the county judge ruled that the body of one missing child was in the vehicle at the time of the crash, so a death certificate was signed on him as well. Toxicology results showed that Jennifer's blood alcohol content was over the limit; Sarah and two children had Benadryl in their bodies. Sarah had made Google searches about "the lethality of Benadryl" and "the nature of death by drowning"; her searches also included "No-kill shelters for dogs," as the family had two pets; apparently, this suicide had been planned in advance. It showed that Sarah told her co-worker that she wished someone told, "It is okay not to have a big family." Wiki

31

shows that the couple had been struggling with and physically abusing their children for years.

I think it was very *noble* for the couple to adopt orphans, initially; it's one way to take care of kids who need help without increasing our population. Still, I think they should have granted that taking care of children is extremely hard: *No reason to go too ambitious about it.* I know this adoption case is different from producing too many babies, as there are people having so many children no matter what (particularly low income or Latin Americans). After the success of "*Jon and Kate plus 8*" TV shows, there are more couples giving birth to sextuplets and putting them on TV these days.

Personally, **I don't consider producing a lot of babies as an *accomplishment***; especially, there is nothing much for men to do to make that happen; at least, women have to go through pregnancy and labor, but what does a man need to do exactly? Eating a lot of food is not an achievement; sleeping for long is not an attainment. From a point of view, all of these are just results caused by irresponsibilities due to not controlling basic instincts.

* * *

I watched a documentary about poor senior citizens in Korea the other day; it reported that suicide rate in the country is the highest among OECD[5]s in the past two decades; this has happened, especially among the elderly after retirements. They interviewed a grandpa who had

---

[5] Organization for Economic Co-operation and Development – 38 wealthiest countries in the world.

been a construction painter for life. He lived in a small room in a decaying residence and said he watches TV all day and eats a small rice porridge twice a day purchased from a convenience store; he and his wife had raised three children there, though they all moved out as adults. Suddenly, this idea hitted me: "*If he had only one child instead of three, could things have been better?*" I am experiencing now that it costs a lot to raise one. Subsequently, I have wondered, "Korea is super crowded now – more every year. Was it necessary for him to have even one?" The human population is increasing fast everywhere on Earth now: **More than ever**. This may be something we need to consider before moving on to the next stage.

In my opinion, having too many children *blindly* can be a sin; at least, I would say it can be very selfish, as **our survival heavily depends on the death of other animals.** As much as our lives are important, their lives matter, too. I strictly do not eat chicken, but it shows that over 50 billion chickens are slaughtered every year; other animals are butchered as well, including cows, pigs, sheep, goats, ducks, fishes, etc; certainly, livestock are not the only ones killed by humans.

Human population is expected to be over 9.2 billion by 2040, according to the Director of National Intelligence: It means **over 1 billion more humans will be created and added on top of the current in the next 17 years;** this is an extremely fast increase in any standard. People often suffer when they give birth and raise children physically or financially; I don't see a visible need for us to go through more pains while struggling.

I saw an Indonesian lady's video on YouTube the other day. She was the wife of a Korean man and it seemed the couple had made tons of foods on a regular basis and donated them to poor children in Bali; it was supposed to be humanitarian. One day, the couple bought a fat pig (150 lb.) to kill and cook. I do not know why, but the lady was so elated with a big smile and tried to carry the pig with giggling and laughter with villagers, while the pig was screaming to death – *such a horrific scream.* I felt disgusted by her mindset: "Only humans matter and nothing else." I think we ought to change our attitudes: **Humans won't last long by being offensive:** Changing our views may be the ultimate way we can make our survival a little longer.

* * *

There is a movie titled *Brokeback Mountain* starring Gyllenhaal and Ledger; G was the rich and L was the poor. There was a restaurant scene in the movie; poor L said, "You forgot what it's like being *broke* all the time. Have you ever heard of child support?" The rich had one child and the poor had three children (2 girls and 1 stepchild). There is a legendary old tale called *Heung-bu story* in Korea; there are two brothers in the story; the old is rich and the younger is poor. The rich did not have a child, but the poor had nine. Here is a question: *Do we need to have a lot of children from this era?*

It shows the human population was about 300 million in the year of 1 (AD 1^6), according to *8 Billion and Counting* by Scuibba. Now it is about 8 billion in 2023, which

---

[6] When Jesus Christ was born.

represents 7% of the total population of humans ever born on Earth; she wrote that about 108 billion people have been born and died throughout evolution. Along with DNI, the U.N. also projected that the human population will be over 9 billion by 2040 – *more than an exponential growth.* For sure, this explosion has never happened on this planet before. Delivering and raising a child is hard work for everyone, requiring a lot of sacrifices, too. When we sacrifice ourselves, I think someone (else) should get benefit out of it, at least: Do you agree? Otherwise, all of our sacrifices will go in vain. Yet have you ever thought that **no one gets benefit out of our rapid population growth?** What if we sacrifice for nothing? Is it possible that the Earth gets hurt or resources are depleted faster not "in spite of", but "because of" our stupid *"sacrifice?"*

* * *

Have you ever thought that having too many kids in a family can be a reason for a divorce? No one claims this, but it's highly likable, according to my experience; it is important since people file bankruptcies largely because of divorces. I *used to* wonder why some parents get divorced, long after having three kids; it takes several years for a couple to have multiple kids; I thought that they would have known each other well enough, before having that many. Now, as a parent, I can reasonably suspect that *having too many kids itself may be the reason for a divorce*: For example, it is statistically true that **mothers with twins have higher rates of divorces than one in America**; the rate gets even higher when parents have bigger multiplets. I believe that every marriage can be greatly different, depending on the number of children a family has.

In a sense, I feel that getting married is similar to getting a job, especially for women, who are about to be full-time housewives. If we suppose a housewife is a job, it can be heaven to hell, depending on the number of kids; to me, taking care of only one has been an enormous amount of work. Certainly, marriage life can be hell to heaven *based on a lot of things*: The difference is that we can still decide and control how many kids we have, at least. We can inherit hardships from our parents, which often we cannot control. Still, in my case, I was able to decide how many kids I can have: **We don't have to create hardships for ourselves, when we have a choice.**

Do you know how to avoid a divorce? From *my point of view as a husband,* it is crucial that the home should be a *livable* and *workable place* for a wife. In other words, I believe a pleasant marriage means the amount of work in a household should be doable; at least, it shouldn't be a hellish amount, especially for a wife. Otherwise, it is more probable that she feels like giving it up. At least, those feelings happened to me in my previous jobs and businesses.

Certainly, a wife can still stay and do large amounts of work without complaining, even when her husband brings meager wages to home: *But why is this necessary?* What if we have a choice to make situations easier? Isn't it better for a wife to get little amounts of work? Isn't it *even better* if she does those while her husband is rich? Less women will file divorces in better conditions. When we think about it, **the job of a housewife is not strikingly different from jobs outside.** I think it is husbands' judgment to create livable conditions for wives and avoid divorces.

Imagine your home is a restaurant; in a point of view, home is a place to make and serve foods. Then, which restaurant would you like to work at? A or B?

A

B

(Image source: random free photos online)

If the two households have the same incomes, I would choose "A." Some restaurants have a crazy amount of customers with a lot of work to do; still, when owners pay employees well with benefits, many laborers stay, despite hellish amounts of work; these are usually upscale restaurants.

In another type, pay is barely minimum, but they have a small amount of work to do. I have seen employees stay for decades in this type of restaurant; these places are often in big hospitals or nursing homes, as a huge medical facility can have several restaurants inside. I used to work in one of those only for breakfast for months; that was the *easiest job* I ever had, because not many eat breakfasts compared with lunch or dinner. Unless caring for more salary, working there only four hours in the morning was ideal for me; the management didn't care much about sales or the number of guests eating; the facility made money out of caregiving, instead. I think my current home is similar to this situation: I cannot bring a huge income, yet my wife has less things to do with a child.

On the other hand, most restaurants on the streets don't (can't) pay employees a lot, while having too much work to do. So many servers quit on a weekly basis there; employee turnover is high and labor shortages are constant in those. I believe most families (60%), having wives with jobs and two children, are in this condition; the high employee quitting rates are similar to the high divorce rates in America. Conclusively, the most ideal option for a wife is that she gets paid a lot, while having a tiny amount of work. Still, a poor husband like me can try to make the condition that his wife has little things to do, even though he cannot bring a lot of money home: *Planning wisely from the start could be cheaper than going through divorces.* Then, how can I decrease the amount of work for my wife? One way is having fewer babies – one in my case. Here is a question, though: **What blocks you from having *less* babies?** Personally, I do not see a disadvantage when my wife has less chores; frankly, I feel less guilty when I know that she's having a hard time with one, instead of more.

* * *

I honestly do not know how others can take care of more than *one* child. I used to take my daughter everywhere by the time she got into elementary: libraries, zoos, museums, aquariums, restaurants, malls, etc. I spent plenty of time with her outside during the summers and felt good about myself – *what a great dad I am!* "I am such a great husband to give my wife enough time to take a rest." Unfortunately, it did *not last* very long; I think I got exhausted after doing that for a few years.

Now it has been several years that only my wife has taken care of my daughter exclusively; I have gotten too tired; I just do not have energy any more to play with my daughter, not to mention bring her out, which actually requires a lot of energy when we think about it. Fortunately, we have a nice young lady next door and my daughter spends time with her frequently; more luckily, her mother visited this summer and brought my daughter out to the farmer's market the other day, too. So I would say that four adults take care of a child now and it seems it really takes a village to raise a child. I am not sure if I am particularly bad with child rearing – all I know is I am very tired.

I think raising a child is hard in two aspects – physical and financial. I just mentioned the physical part, but it costs a lot, too. I am from a wealthy family and got multiple financial support from my parents, but the cost has not been as cheap as I expected in the beginning of 2010. One question to myself, though: *Is it necessary to go through more of this hardship?* **Does anyone get a benefit out of my repetition?** No and *No one* really does. It is just our instinct to leave an offspring; no one seems to get particular benefits out of overpopulation.

I have detested crowded places. I was not peculiarly like this when I was young. But after I became 40, I started hating crowdedness and loud noises more each year. During the COVID quarantine in 2021, I was happy to be in our library alone, as I was virtually the only one in the building; others did not get out of their houses as much. I literally experienced from hell to heaven in the same spot. That is why I believe a country like Bangladesh is anguished: **Not only because of poverty, more because of crowdedness.**

* * *

Currently, I am reading *12 Rules for Life* by Peterson. It's a top seller, but only *theoretically* well written in my opinion – no *practical* solutions. It shows that the author has been a Harvard professor for 30 years; not many people are in that position and I felt his suggestions are not realistic, especially to the middle 50% in our society. The book starts with a story about lobsters, which have been on Earth for over 400 million years. He explained that even they have a sense of social hierarchy deep in their brains; every animal has the sense instinctively, including humans. So he suggested that it is important for us to "stand up straight with our shoulders back." Apparently, this straight posture shows others the sign of a winner and will prevent possible conflicts with them. This may be a great scientific point, but wrong solution.

As he explained, Earth has too many animals, but too few ideal shelters and resources for them. That is why fighting happens everywhere all the time – in classrooms, Ukrainian borders or wherever. According to the book, after fighting, the winners stand up straight and the losers shrink their postures; it says that this has happened throughout history on Earth. So is showing bossy a good solution? I still believe that everyone gets hurt one way or another in fighting.

I think the better solution is that **we should learn how to give up for more after having enough.** I think that is what intelligent *Homo sapiens* should do; otherwise, there is no difference between men and lobsters. I believe having a showy posture may be effective to defend ourselves, at most; keeping the dominating posture, being competitive or working harder is not the answer; we will only get injured more if we keep exposing ourselves in conflicts. I think we should lessen greedy attempts, if there is no point getting more; we are not the robin as in the book. It is time to think differently, as modern humans who have evolved from the original *Sapiens* 300,000 years ago – no point to kill each other as *Australopithecus* had 4 million years ago.

People often put themselves in danger not because they need something, but because they want more: **Greed is the enemy.** While a few are excellent at keeping in good posture, others lose: these triumph and defeat cycles have caused misery for all of us; everyone loses this way in the end. **We should learn how to stop when enough is**

enough; we should control ourselves to make things better for everyone, including every animal, plant or other life on Earth. Unpleasantly, most books have been written to benefit only humans.

I remember Peterson was once on a talk show and the host asked, "How many children is ideal for a family?" He directly answered, "I don't think one is a good number." He said children can learn from each other when parents have *two* kids – nonsense as families do not live separately in a prison cell. I think he answered "two" since he has two. Or two is fine since Canada, where he lives, is totally empty. I don't think we can expect practical advice from an Ivy professor for average fathers who worry about daycare tuition. I strongly believe one child *at most* a family is the way to go. Earth will be super crowded in the end, which *can trigger extinction faster.* **Not reaching the next stage of overpopulation is for both humans and other lives on Earth.**

* * *

The summary so far: "Having a lot of babies is the number one reason for poverty and social problems. Earth is already crowded and depleting enough that no one needs to have more than one child any more. 1.2 billion of the new population will be generated by 2040, so poor people don't have to try hard." We all know that humans have caused miseries on other humans; people talk about Jewish holocaust or African slavery. However, did you notice that tons of animals are born to live only a couple of months and *butchered*? We can be vegetarians to help them. Or more ultimately, we can have fewer babies, too.

The human population will be over 9 billion, regardless if I have one or two; one more baby can contribute to killing an extra 100 chickens – a meal issue for us, but a life or death matter for them. Simultaneously, I am glad I have only one since I have been less stressed out financially. Conclusively, **I believe that having fewer babies is a win-win situation**: Good for my stress relief, chickens and the Earth's environment, including limited resources.

In a sense, no one *needs* to have a baby any more: **No animal on Earth has such an obligation, to begin with.** My daughter was born when I still owned the video game store, which was small (900 sf) in 2010. I barely made a monthly rent of $1,200 then, so I could not hire any employee throughout the eight years. My wife taught at a music school two days a week, which was located in a music store. She was so popular that her schedules were all booked completely from morning till evening (no lunch break) for those two days; I heard that, rarely, some artists didn't have a single student there.

I had double duties on those two days: taking care of my store and *baby daughter* together. We set up a baby room with the "pack and play" crib from Greco in the back. I had a hard time whenever a good amount of customers flooded in, all at once. That had happened all along for the last four years of my store life. We never knew what would happen 10 minutes later in that place – empty or crowded. I was busy with eBay sales[7], too.

---

[7] A top rated seller since 2003.

The store had a big screen TV for video games; I used to watch reality shows like "Jon and Kate plus 8" or "Nineteen plus counting." I was curious how others can take care of 6 identical babies or 19 kids in a family. Taking care of only one had been more than a struggle for me (still *one* is hard, even though my wife takes care of her most). Eventually, I think humans have conquered the Earth and become the most dominant species. On a large scale, it is devastating that the top of the food chain is getting bigger. Most conflicts happen fundamentally because too many people share too little resources. On a personal scale, once we have a baby, we generally face two problems; firstly, we cannot work ourselves since we have to take care of the baby. Secondly, our spending becomes double for the baby while we cannot work as before.

* * *

Like many of you, I had pressure to have two babies in my 30s. It came from everywhere: parents, wife, friends, TV, social media, etc. Physically, I was able to do so. But I am glad I have stuck to my own opinion and managed not to have more. In fact, having only one child turned out to be the best decision I have made, after all. I closed out my video game store when the lease was over in 2014. I took a break for 1 year and found a job in the nursing home nearby in 2015. After working at the nursing home for 7 years, I decided to resign in 2022. The place had been worse every year and eventually filed Chapter 11 bankruptcy in 2023 – its kitchens had so much food waste all the time. I started the weekend dishwasher job as they requested, which was fine only in the first 2 years. Then, a horrible Mexican sous chef Carl came and things got unnecessarily stressful.

I tried to transfer to other departments after getting a medical coder license in 2018, which didn't work out for gender discrimination I suspect. The director of health information was a snobbish, unpleasant woman; I noticed that all the workers and receptionists in that department were women (*every single one of them*). I did not make a big deal, since it was not a high paying job or pleasant place to work, anyway; I learned that the woman director was fairly obnoxious during the job interview. I could see why so many women quit that seemingly easy job. Moreover, I believe that I was overqualified with certificates, which were not required. It was nonsense for me to try hard to share an awkward time with the witch boss.

COVID arrived two years later and the dishwashers got even shorter in the nursing home after 2020. I tried to transfer to a wait staff only to avoid the horrid sous chef, but it did not work out again for any reason I could understand. I had worked two positions for the last 8 months of my employment there: the weekend dishwasher and weekday morning waiter; I was not able to transfer to the wait staff completely for any reason. I felt it seems the entire managers in that nursing home tried to force me to be a dishwasher since it was severely short.

Finally, a new company came and took over only the entire dining department in 2022; I did not know there was a transfer deadline to the new company. I was scheduled to take a pharmacy technician exam around that time, which I passed at the first try. I told them I can still work as a dishwasher only on Sunday if they still need me. They said the transfer deadline had passed and suggested a slightly lower hourly rate; I am glad that I wrote a resignation letter and quit. It was a bad job in many senses: toxic chemicals to my skin (possibly cancer causing), low quality managers, etc. Truthfully, I have been wealthy enough not to get any job at all by then; my investments have been successful all along; I have not been in a situation to need a job or to earn certificates.

Still, do you know what I was glad the most when I decided to get out of the nursing home completely? Having enough savings? Getting dividends and interest to cover my expenses? Having earned two certificates? My wife has been working all along? Above all, **I was glad the most that I have only one child to support.** During the 7 years, I had witnessed that good guys stuck in that dreadful job. Joe and Riccardo had four kids each – these two were nice guys, but had worked for two different jobs. I feel truly sorry for them since the working environment there was hostile, harmful and unfair – *hell created by humans.*

We may start seeing more career changes from now, as people live longer. When people lived only until 60, I assume that people never really changed their professions and passed away right after retirement. Soon, the average Joe like you and me will live up to 100; having a career change can be more common. Number of kids we need to feed will matter whenever we change our jobs for any reason: job loss, economic depression, better positions, ambitions, etc.

* * *

I think hardships have two types: *given and created*. If we are born in a poor family or have a sick mother to take care of, these are *given* hardships. But if you create four children and struggle to support them, those are hardships created by you. We can have hardship – **we do not have to create one.** There was a woman cook named Roza in the kitchen of the nursing home; she was a Cuban Mexican single mother with a lot of tattoos and piercings; I never liked her since she was always *disrespectful* to dishwashers. She had a mother with liver cancer and five children to support (three different fathers). **Her sick mother is a given hardship; her five kids were a hardship created by herself**; I heard her complaining about money multiple times.

Still her action to create more kids could be beneficial for our society, right? Not necessarily. I recall that she eventually got fired in 2018; I believe the reason was drug addiction. I guess she probably has taken welfare checks since her Facebook showed she had been at home all the time with two toddlers; it's not necessarily advantageous for tax collection. And her children can be troublemakers later on, as the mother was not sane – building more prisons can be another tax loss. In conclusion, I don't believe her actions to create five kids was inevitably favorable for society.

Nonetheless, are her children happy, at least? I doubt it since they had been without fathers or enough money all along. Conclusively, producing five kids might not be optimal for her own wellbeing, society or even children themselves. I don't think any baby wants to be born in that family – there is no romance in poverty. No one gets benefit, while Earth gets exponentially crowded these days.

Life is harsh already – true for all the animals on Earth. I used to think that whatever happens in our lives is mostly luck, which is probable only until we become 20. Now, at the age of 49, I can say **we are the ones who decide our own destinies.** *Having a hard time ourselves doesn't necessarily mean others get benefit out of it* – we can make our life grueling or we don't have to. At least, we can make some choices.

* * *

Summary

1. We don't have to push ourselves to have a lot of children any more.
2. Regardless of whether I have one or two, the human population will be 9 billion soon. I know I could have had a way harder time if I had two.
3. We don't have to sacrifice ourselves to deplete resources faster.

3

Getting into Debt Too Easily

If money is a religion, debt is a cult.
-Brad Kong

I believe getting a debt happens *when stupidity meets greed*; smart but greedy people don't have debt; the stupid but humble never have it, either. However, the stupid but greedy get it. Believe it or not, not paying a debt used to be a felony; it was common to go to prison for it in Europe. People still go to court when they file a bankruptcy: Why? It used to be a crime. I use my two credit cards everywhere, though I have always paid up my balance; I admit that we cannot live without them, although the reason has been convenience for me. Still, it's worth thinking one more time before signing up for a big one like a mortgage – basically, people can pay more for the same things, after all.

There is a book titled *Debt: The First 5000 Years* by Graeber. It explains that debt was invented during the Sumer civilization in Mesopotamia[8] about 3,500 B.C. I would say that the concept of debt is recent since it was formed only 5,500 years ago. Humans started farming only about 10,000 years ago, despite that we have been on Earth up to six million years. It has been normal for humans not to have any debt during most of history.

---

[8] South central region of Iraq in 2023.

I think that the smartest thing I did *with money* was buying my condo *"in full"* in 2013. I know it is hard, especially when we live in the east or west regions in America; typically, the house prices there are three times higher than in the Midwest where I live. In 2008, the subprime mortgage crisis broke out and I recall it had lasted about five years. A huge amount of foreclosures and short sales came out on the market and these dropped housing prices significantly. By then, I had lived in rental apartments for about fourteen years. I had about $80,000 emergency fund my parents gave me after my daughter was born, all of which I saved in CDs at the bank initially. The price of a one-bedroom condo tanked to $60,000, so I bought it quickly.

One *advantage* when we buy a home in full is a *discount.* The nice Polish couple owners[9] said they had two houses and were in need of cash. I got a $5,000 discount[10] immediately when I suggested a cash payment. I used to pay $900 a month for apt rent by 2013 (a one bedroom rent is about $1,500 a month in Chicagoland, as of 2024). Now I pay about $395 HOA fee (association fee) a month, so I believe I am saving about $1,000 a month; which makes the annual saving $10,000 a year after deducting $2,000 property tax I pay, as a condo owner. I have lived here close to 12 years now, so probably $120,000 has been saved only by not having a rent. I will save even more if I stay here longer.

---

[9] I am glad they removed the stove in this unit, which was a fire hazard and makes this 850 sf condo even smaller. Without them, I wouldn't have known that we have an option.

[10] The original *listing* price was $65,000 in 2013.

It shows that the average lifespan of males is 78 years in America in 2024. I felt it's too much to spend 30 years only on paying mortgages in that sense – it's like spending most of adult lives on paying a house. I could have gone for a two-story house with a mortgage in 2012; I am glad that I didn't. In general, housing costs much more with debts. More importantly, I couldn't have been a writer if I had chosen that option; I could have worked for a medical coder full-time, which I do not care about, only to pay a home loan. *I just couldn't let myself waste three decades that way.*

* * *

Debts are everywhere these days: a mortgage, car loan or credit card – the major three types. Personally, I do not have any of those. I am using two cards all the time, but the balances are always close to $0 at the end of month. It is not like I am rich – I just don't spend a lot. Slavery from Africa might have been over 200 years ago; now geniuses have created a new serf system. **In this brilliant set-up, slaves do not even know that they are ones.** It doesn't even matter if you are a black, white or yellow; if we are poor, financially illiterate or *frequently both*, you just get sucked in. Some are willing to wait in line for hours to get into the traps; some show off they are in ones. Rarely, I wonder if some *internet trolls* don't know how to use a calculator, *'They must haven't graduated elementary.'* **We pay more for the same <u>with debt</u>;** some gnomes were even proud to have mortgages since they believe that everyone in the world has it; statistics show only 60% of Americans have them.

I argue that there is nothing really worth trying with debt. I obviously know we need to use debt somehow during our lifetimes. But this idea should be the basic: **No debt if possible.** Debt has had a lot of different names: balance, credit, margin, remainder, etc – these are merely fancy names of leftover, business, investment and card debt, which make us feel better or confused. Having debt used to be considered terrible decades ago; it has become a natural part of our lives these days. I have never paid any interest on my cards for a decade now; in fact, I get cash backs from both every month; my spending limits are about $18,000 from both combined. I had a car loan 9 years ago, but the 3-year loan was paid off within 3 months in 2014.

* * *

It is proven that people cannot focus on their jobs when they have worries: How do we get them constantly? One way is having a debt, which will distract us regularly, so we can make less money in the end. How can we know if our lives are going in a positive direction? In my opinion, there are a couple of barometers to check that straight: our weights and debts. Are you lean? If so, more likely your life is in a good position, as no one gets skinny automatically these days – foods are cheap and everywhere. Weight loss requires controls and disciplines. Less likely you will spend a lot on medical bills in the future; this is a sign that our lives are headed in a better direction.

The other indicator is our debt situation in my opinion; frankly, having any type of debt is not very good news, to begin with. Do you own a home outright without having a mortgage or rent? Then, definitely your life has been constructive so far – you might not be rich yet, but on the way. Paying for a house in full requires financial knowledge, savings, luck and having strong wills, as some get mortgages blindly. **While smart people try to hide their wealths, stupids *pretend* to have them with debt** (for example, some buy luxury cars with auto loans); this is purely idiotic from a perspective. I know a couple of Korean mothers whose children got kidnapped after pretending to be affluent[11]. Regardless, showing-off can offend others for no reason, while some lose money on loan interests themselves.

Unfortunately, I never have had an amicable relationship with my father. But I admit that he has been right about one thing: **No debt.** He frequently said to me and my brother that, "Your dad does not have a debt." He has not been a pleasant person to deal with, but his voice changed tenderly whenever he mentioned this. What he meant by "debt" was "business debt," by the way. Not using a debt to buy a house or car was out of the question to him (he always used full cash). If you know about old Korean men, you will understand it better. What can I say? *He is the one who made $20 M from scratch.* Those old Koreans did not have anything, since the Korean war totaled the country 70 years ago; South Korea was a ruin 60 years ago just like Ukraine in 2024. While most Koreans are not as rich as my father, it seems the "no debt" policy seemed to work out for him.

I found a Buddhist maxim online the other day: "Pain is not holding you; you are the one holding the pain. If you cannot save yourself, no one can. We are the result of the thought in the past – we will become the person in our thinking." The Dalai Lama also once said, "Humans are

---

[11] The movie *Secret Sunshine* is based on true stories.

created to be loved and stuff are created to be used. Stuff are being loved and humans are being used nowadays." I think this applies to materialism in general, but especially true to cars and houses.

* * *

There was a Korean internet community I used to browse; trolls there were stupid, spending-wise. It seemed they all made traditional and boring financial mistakes – very typical lives, including full time jobs, mortgages, car loans, two cars, *two* children, wives with *no* job, etc. I had never expected a maverick there, but I was amazed at how they live so monotonously without any twist at all. Funny thing was that some tried to argue with me, despite the fact that they all pay double on their house through their mortgages.[12] There is nothing wrong with it technically, as using a mortgage is reasonable when even the cheapest houses are too expensive (i.e., in San Francisco); trolls there shouldn't have argued that getting debt is better than cash payment. In the community, I saw that some bought big houses with the hope that their house prices spark up someday. Currently, the single[13] population is increasing faster and less likely they will buy big houses. I honestly don't think that all the house tags go up more than inflation, but probably condo prices will increase faster, as the single prefer and can afford small units.

Most of us get debts unconsciously. I think a majority become frugal after being burned by a debt somehow. I

---

[12] It is mathematically true that people often pay their house close to double with 30-year mortgages.
[13] People who are not married.

used to be a big waster myself, especially during the time I owned a business; during the *Cyb Knight* period, I remember that I owed up to $9,000 credit card debt once in 2009; it was a business debt, not really from personal consumption, though. My mother saved me once and I have never had the same problem again so far. I live frugally even without a car now.

I believe that the second biggest reason why people cannot quit a horrid job is keeping a persistent debt – probably, mortgage is the most common. To me, buying a big house to show off could be a worse reason than having multiple kids, which is probably the #1 reason to force us to put up with a hellish job. **Debt will never bring us a profit.** I read some trolls declaring that living in a bigger house means better quality of life – this is stupid. **Bigger houses only guarantee that we need to do more chores** – we may or may not be happier, as houses can turn into a nightmare, too; some building problems are impossible to fix. In reality, I would say debt can seriously lower our quality of life. Please trust me that nothing is more important than peace of mind.

* * *

Summary

1. No debt as possible.
2. Not having a debt had been perfectly *normal* in history.
3. See if you can buy a small house in full – getting a complete homeownership has been a life changing experience for me.

4

Not Using Systems Already Paid For

We should use what we already paid first.
-Brad Kong

There is a group of movies titled the *007 series* (*James Bond* films) – the first one was "*Dr. No*" released in 1962. Since then, 24 more have been directed by 2021; the last one was *No Time to Die* starring Craig. There are thousands of action movies released every year and unfortunately, most fail commercially. Still, if a movie comes with a prefix title of 007, it beats the competition and gets millions of audiences. The similar examples are *Mission: Impossible* or *Harry Potter* series. I think an obvious example to use systems they already built is franchising.

The same goes for books. One of my favorite writers, Bryson, has written 19 books by 2023. Oddly, it doesn't seem any of his books have a relation to each other; one is about his childhood and another is about the universe or human body. In my opinion, he could have made more sales if he had arranged these in a type of franchise; for example, universe and body could be in *Bryson's science* series I and II. When readers see II in a book title, they automatically assume there is I, which is an automatic advertisement without spending extra. Besides, some fans have obsessions to collect everything in a series and complete them. Only a portion of authors do this, even though many have published multiple books. In worse cases, some authors don't even use the same pen name. At least, Bryson used *the same name*, so people can find all of his works by searching it. I think we can apply this concept of "using what we already made" to our personal finances, too; in fact, some are broke since they don't do it.

* * *

I think I am a library *maniac* by nature; I have visited more than 30 libraries in Chicagoland so far. While the one in Schaumburg is probably the best here, I found every library has its own ups and downs. One of my sanctuaries is the one in Wheelings – hidden, but the new building is full of modern features. I like the one in Mount Prospect, as it has the latest bestsellers from Korea; sometimes, I wonder who manages the section since all were carefully chosen; I feel the curator actually read those. The one in Arlington Heights has decent interiors; it's also near multiple restaurants in the downtown of the village. The one in Oak park has a huge comic section; the building has five stories and the entire second floor is dedicated to graphic novels. If you are Korean by chance, I think you must visit the one in Glenview and Harold Washington in downtown Chicago; these two have massive amounts of Korean books and I think only libraries in Korea have more than these two.

(Image source: Starfield Library)

The point is that **only *some* of us go to libraries, while *all* of us have paid for them with property taxes.** I used to work at a nursing home, which is only a quarter mile away from the library I visit frequently; the work hired about 1,000 employees. Strangely, I have never run into any of my coworkers there in the last decade (mostly cooks or servers). Actually, in this case, maybe I should say that I was lucky; meeting them could have been awkward, since not everyone from the job was pleasant. Still, you know what, though? *Maybe they still work there since they never go to the library*, which clearly helped me get two new certificates[14].

By the way, do you know how I am certain that all of us paid for the library *already*? Some may think that they are renting apartments, so have never paid property tax, part of which goes to the libraries. **Apartment rents[15] already include any type of property tax** – a portion of rent is

---

[14] Medical coder and pharmacy technician.
[15] Apartment rent = property tax + rental company profit

always property tax of the building without exception. Regardless, **there are people spending money "first," no matter what**, unconsciously. *I think it is more logical to use "everything free" first and spend money if that is not enough.* For example, some people check the library first, if there is a new movie coming out. But others check Redbox *first* to rent or go to Amazon to buy it; I think it is reasonable to do those, if it's not available for free.

* * *

We have paid millions of things already, while we don't notice – **some never use those and spend extra money, being unaware of them.** Whenever I see my property tax bills, I can find a good portion that always goes to the community college nearby. There are students, including myself, going to a four-year university straight from high school, instead of finishing general courses in the community college; which was already paid by their parents who are homeowners or apt renters. That's fine, but I try to make a point that we have paid for something altogether and some do not use it.

Also, on the bills, I saw that nearly $3 billion goes to the water supply in our country each year; they spend extreme amounts on ensuring the quality of water delivered to homes. However, some of us still order water from Hinckley or buy it at Jewel with additional charges: *Spending double all the time could be the reason for brokeness.* I used to buy millions of water bottles from Sam's club, especially while I owned my business. Now I carry a glass bottle to use drinking fountains at libraries, malls or hotels, whose aquatic duct system we all already paid for. Another example is public transportation. Chicago homeowners reading property tax bills must find a chunk of the budget to go to public transits: subways, trains, buses, etc. Yet there are Chicagonians only driving a car as their sole ride. On top of the transportation charges they already paid for, they spend extra money on cars: loans, insurances, registrations, parking, gas, repairs, washings, maintenance, etc. It's *double spendings*; one is on public transportations via property taxes and the other is on cars. Some cannot live without a car for jobs (e.g., delivery guys, construction workers, etc); most of us grab the car key without thought.

Whenever I check my property tax bill, I see that only about $1 M goes to our library every six months; I have always thought that it's just too small out of $6 B. The library has played a crucial role for this community as a true town square for villagers; they have done fabulous jobs, especially compared with others. I insist that they deserve at least $5 M a year, which could be still tiny since over $12 B are collected in this county every year. It is nonsense that the park district gets over $100 millions, while the library only gets $1 M.

* * *

Another example could be the trolleys in this village. We have a big shopping mall area near my home; there are *free* trolleys connecting major spots: Woodfield mall, Street of Woodfield, Ikea, hotel convention center, etc. Many do not use those, and only drive their own cars; I am the only passenger in the clean transit, nine out of ten times. Without them, everyone has to go through more traffic and parking jams as the area is crowded. We had the COVID pandemic for three years by 2022. The federal government sent us stimulus checks, then; some never got those since they didn't file taxes properly – missing the $3,500 checks which they could have gotten legally.

The last example would be the swimming pool in my condo complex; we have a large one right in front of my unit. I have paid for the pool through the HOA association fee every month in the past 11 years. Honestly, I have never used it myself, which has been a waste. But, after my family moved back in 2017, my daughter has stayed there up to 10 hours a day every summer. I think it is smarter to use it, instead of going to a village pool with paying a $10 fee. Actually, local friends can come here for free, but some go to Atlantis in the Bahamas with paying air tickets. **Unfortunately, what they get could be more stress and waiting in lines –** lines for concierges, airports, rental cars, etc.

How can we be wealthy if we keep spending money double all the time? Chicagoland has myriad CTA[16] and Metra stations, and bus stops; not only free trolleys, there are also free vans for seniors. It is walkable with all those public transportations and uber, so my family has lived without a car since 2017. If we are short of money, despite working, we may need to check if there is a spot we spend *double* on. There is a reason why, when your income melts away like snow in the summer breeze.

* * *

Summary

1. Do not spend money *first* for everything.
2. Check if there is something you already paid for.

---

[16] Subway.

3. See if you can plan in advance to save.

5

Double Spending Lifestyle

If we are short of money, while working "full-time,"
something must be wrong from the bottom.
-Brad Kong

Anders Hansen is a psychiatry specialist from the Karolinska Institute in Sweden. He accepted 100 volunteers before 2016 and conducted an experiment; he let 50 people do one-hour walking exercise three times a week for 12 months; he let the other 50 people do only stretching exercise without walking. When he checked their brains, the result was striking: Hippocampus in the brains of walking people increased +2% on average while those of stretching-only people shrank -1%. He suggested that **walking helps our brains grow, regardless of age and limits the dementias.**

What do you believe makes us walk less? Driving. Most Americans spend practically fortunes on cars – including buying, fueling, repairing, cleaning, etc. Then, many spend savings *again* on dementia treatments later in their lives. **This is a *double spending*** in a sense: car and hospital costs. *Is it possible if we live without a car and walk for brain health,* from the start? Then, it's *double saving* – saving from "not owning a car" and "not staying in a memory care," when we get old. Some buy doughnuts, eat them and go to dentists. Or others do not buy a doughnut from the start and do not go for implants as much. **I noticed some spend double or triple all the time for the same results.**

I believe those *who spend double* live rather on emotion than logic. Let's assume everyone goes to the library everyday; I live about 1 mile from one in our town. I always go there by walking and it takes about 25 minutes, which is a good exercise itself. However, I notice that some go to the library by car, gym by car, spend money on gym membership and then do walking exercises there. **It is *quadruple* spending for the same result: gas consumption; gym memberships and clothings; electricity on treadmills, etc.** Similarly, a lot of people go to work by car and go jogging after work: Why don't they just ride bicycles to work from the start, so they can save on gas and don't have to run after work?

On the contrary, I witnessed some smart people do their hobbies at work. When I was in downtown Chicago, I saw a construction site near the Willis tower; they were building a ground expansion of the skyscraper. For an hour, I had observed how the tips of new building frames were connected manually[17]. What struck me was a muscular guy trying to connect two huge beams by hand; he seemed to be the type going to the gym everyday; apparently, his job also provided him plenty of things to lift the whole day; he seemed to pursue his passion during work outside the gym as well. Another example is the Bloomingdale trail in Chicago, which is a walking bridge; I saw myriads of people go to work by bicycles or kick scooters.

* * *

---

[17] There is no other way.

I wonder how carnivores were created originally; it must be painful for them to survive; they have to kill others, whenever they need to eat; this is an offensive way to live on Earth. On the contrary, the lives of herbivores or omnivores seem to be less harsh, as plants they feed on don't move. In this sense, the creatures living in the least offensive way could be scavengers; they just eat whenever anything edible is found. I read that lobsters, living on the ocean floor, eat debris dropped from the surface; it's an example of living in the least offensive way. I believe this is how they have survived for more than 400 million years – by **not bothering others, and being helpful to clean environments.**

Modern humans are abusively wasteful; we have the most offensive way of lifestyle on Earth. It is not like poor people are frugal, while the rich are lavish – we all are *prodigal* to some points. We do not see animals like humans *in the wild: Why?* **Wasteful ones must have been extinct already.** Nature does not allow animals from being thriftless – humans will be no exception. Our agriculture started 10,000 years ago at the earliest. If humans become extinct within the next 100,000 years, that is not a long survival span for a species; dinosaurs had lived through for over 165 million years on Earth, which are still alive as birds. I agreed with a joke from a biology book: If aliens visit Earth a million years later, their description of humans will be *"The shortest, but most impactfully lived species."*

People can live up to 100 years these days. When I checked Wiki, I found a lot of people used to die before 40 even in the 19th century. Some know that the painter, Van Gogh, died at 37; did you know his art dealer brother, who supported him financially, died at 33 as well? As people start living longer, I do *not* think we should live extravagantly any more: In fact, we should live as frugally as possible; otherwise, we may not be able to hang on to our money all the way up until we die at 100. Simply, we are given more years to spend money than our grandparents. When we hear, "an old person died," we automatically assume that he or she passed away naturally. **But it's possible that a portion of poor seniors' deaths can be actual suicides, which are falsely reported as natural deaths.** Statistically, it shows houseless or *van dwellers*[18] die earlier; I suspect death could be the only way for them to *graduate* from their painful lives; in the future, this can be true even for the entire human race on a large scale.

* * *

The weekend dishwasher job at the nursing home was physically hard, especially in the beginning. The place is only a mile from my home and it took about 30 minutes for me to get there by walking. After getting the medical coder license in 2018, I was wondering if I should keep the job or not even for weekends; it was mentally fine without stress in the first few years. I concluded, 'I can consider it as <u>weekend gym exercises</u> for eight hours; the only difference is *I get paid and receive free meals*.' It's true that I have lost a lot of weight and become more muscular after starting the job; I was obese[19] and diabetic before. I had commuted strictly by walking[20] throughout the 7 years to intensify my exercise. **Some spend money to lose weight, while others get paid for the same result.**

It was hard for me to wake up early in the morning, especially during winters. I thought that it would be hard as well, if I had

---

[18] Check *Nomadland* by Bruder.
[19] I used to be up to 165 pounds, but 125 pounds now.
[20] I still had a brand new car for two years after starting that job

to exercise in the gym for 8 hours a day during weekends. **We can skip the gym easily, but cannot be late for work, so the job had been a better coach in a sense.** During the 7 years, there had been extremely cold or snowy days – horrible winters in Chicago. "Well, some go to Mount Everest after spending a fortune; let me consider that I am doing winter climbing in Colorado today." The thirty minute adventures to work didn't look bad relatively – the commutes were over quickly. Additionally, that job has assured me why I should not waste money. I still feel sorry for those doing that for a living, though.

Particularly, I felt sorry for a Mexican boy named Omar, who was in his late 20s; he had done that for a decade only because he was born in a poor family. I used to say to my wife that, *"The only crime he committed was being born in a poor family."* It is sad that **"born destitute" is such a crime to get that kind of punishment**, as the job was painful enough for me to consider it as a penalty, especially over the winters. He was such a noble boy who accepted his hardship without a complaint and helped coworkers feel pleasant. I wish Latinos would not breed blindly, so less children would get punished like that.

When I was in college, there was a Ukrainian girl who had worked at Disney World for a summer. I assume she wanted to have a vacation there, but could not afford it; it seemed smart for her to work there, get paid and enjoy vacation together for about three months. I believe similar things happen in cruise lines as well; if we don't want to spend on cruise travel, we might work there, too. To write this book, I could have hired low incomers and paid them to listen to their stories. I read the graphic novel, "Jungle", originally by Sinclair, about immigrants working in butcheries during the Great Recession; I read their hardship had been intensified after their child was born. It showed in the end that Sinclair actually hired the protagonist in the novel to listen to his story. Alternatively, I think **the author could have worked in a factory himself and collected info for his book while getting paid;** some do the same while making money and others don't. If we keep being short despite working, I think we should check if we spend double on anything, somehow.

* * *

Summary

1. Try to walk, instead of driving; walking can be a gas saving tool, but also a great exercise itself.
2. Try not to spend double for the same results.
3. It would be great if we can choose a workplace where we can use our passion.

This is a bonus for paperback!

6

Living in an Expensive Area

Our evolution speed doesn't catch up with Civilization. -Brad Kong

Statistically, the east and west regions in America are about three times more expensive than the Midwest in terms of housing; I personally don't see a logical advantage to living there – nonsense to pay more to get to wildfires (west) or hurricanes (southeast). It seems to be more sensible to move from the coasts to mid-America, which is actually happening nowadays; Texas, Idaho and South Dakota have gotten the biggest moving-in populations since 2020. I live in Illinois, which is also losing population every year; I believe it's due to high state income and property tax here. However, the Chicagoland part is still growing and I guess I will keep staying here for some reason. First of all, I think the living cost in the Midwest is still *lower,* even after higher taxes. Though not widely known, property taxes are _not high_ for condos in Illinois; I own a condo and it has been less than $2,000 a year after homeowner's exemption.

Secondly, I bought my place during the subprime mortgage meltdown in 2013; I cannot find a residence in a decent neighborhood for that price any more. It's hard to let it go since I know I will never get it back for the same price. Thirdly, the city of Chicago and its vicinity have the third biggest population in America and provided me plenty of places to walk around (walking is my greatest joy). Besides, the city has old, but well established public transportation systems, which helps me live without a car now. I used to have symptoms of diabetes and walking has helped me stay away from them.

I concluded an expensive area may not be a good place to live *by nature*. Let's take Times Square, for instance, which is the most expensive block in America and basically no one resides there. But imagine we can live there for *free*: Is it a nice place to stay? I will suffer from noise, crowds, pollution and bright lights all the time. I know we have to spend more money on rent to live there, yet it doesn't provide us with any optimal conditions we can find easily in the suburbs. Although there is a difference on the discomfort level, I believe *expensive places* might be somewhat like Times Square; there is a reason why a place attracts more people (i.e., scenic views). And living in a crowded place *must* come with discomforts along with more financial burden. Sometimes, I go to downtown Chicago to walk around. I always thought that I would not visit my village if I lived downtown. You know what, though? That is the reason why I feel happier to live in the suburbs. *Since no traveler visits my village, I get more peace and less trouble.*

* * *

Mental comfort is "much more" important than physical one. It was too hot yesterday, as it's in mid-August. I thought I would go to a cooler place, and had two choices: Rolling Meadows library and Barnes and Noble: Which one did I choose? The library. It was all about mental comfort; I could stay in the empty library for hours without

71

caring about others. B&N probably won't say a thing for me to do the same. Still I know I will get sales pressure to buy. Regardless, I just didn't feel comfortable killing time in a place selling something. I believe everyone has his or her own sanctuary. When I think about it, it is mostly about mental comfort. I like RM library simply because no one goes there – clean, but isolated, as most don't know there is such a place. In a sense, outsiders never go there since it is small or does not have anything special – one of the libraries not having a single Korean book. No one likes it, so I feel peaceful there. I like the one in our village, but it is too popular and crowded; people come from everywhere and many of the staff recognize who I am – mentally less comfortable, as I prefer being anonymous.

Most people do not consider this mental comfort *seriously* when they buy a house. I happened to be in our neighbor's unit in this building once and found out that they do not have any trees covering their windows. I felt like I was standing on a stage in front of the audience there. In my unit, three windows are covered by four trees; I always feel laid back and hidden in my unit. In my opinion, *it is not a coincidence that owners change every few years in the neighboring unit.* However, the previous owner in my unit had lived here for 23 years until she passed away.

Since the longer we own a house the more profit we make, it's important to check if we feel comfortable to stay for long before buying a house. Some focus only on checking how the home looks to others: Does it look fancy enough? Some get an awful amount of debt to disguise themselves to look pretty. They actually put themselves in more nervous situations, including getting a thief or collection call from banks after all.

Frankly, I have always thought NYC is the worst place to live in America. At least, I am in a position to judge that, as I graduated from SUNY at Buffalo and had visited NYC more than 30 times before graduation by 2006; the city has a big Korean community, too. My conclusion? Expensive, yet dirty. I had chances to visit dozens of other cities in America for life. According to my experience, most of them were cleaner, cheaper or safer than NYC. A few places are more expensive, but at least it was nicer like old San Francisco. I could have settled in NYC in 2006, if the cost of living was cheaper at least, despite its filths. But *I thought it was absurd to pay more to live in a dirty environment* – getting smaller spaces for higher rents. Whenever I visited there, I always felt its citizens were under more stress. And *I noticed that overcharging came from everywhere from restaurants to bridge tolls.* I had more cloudy weather than sunny during multiple visits. Personally, I have lived in roughly four cities in America in the last 25 years: Rochester, Ithaca and Buffalo, NY; Chicago suburbs, IL. I have never lived in NYC, but eventually, I found out NYC is far more expensive than others – the farther from it, the cheaper.

Have you heard of the "California exodus?" A film shows over 80,000 companies have moved out from CA since 2012, including Tesla, Hewlett Packard, Oracle, etc. They said that the reasons are high cost of living and State income taxes; a lot of those companies have moved to Texas, particularly near the Austin area. There used to be a funny Mexican dishwasher named Vincente at the nursing home I used to work at; he was about 60 and had 5 children; he said three of his children live in CA already. Although I suggested not to, he ended up moving to CA in 2019. I heard he worked in construction there now. Serious wildfires and droughts broke out one by one after he moved to CA, so I wonder if his decision was wise.

There is a Korean community site I used to go to. I got surprised repeatedly, whenever I heard their complaints about the cost of living in CA. An exceptionally large number of people on that site were from Silicon Valley near SF, which is the most expensive city in America as of 2024. Their salaries and house prices they mentioned were unbelievable; I concluded that they probably got paid more, but ended up having nothing in hand as they spent all on mortgages.

There is a travel YouTuber named "Korean Jay." His channel had an episode where he visited a girl's apartment in LA and I was shocked that her rent was $4,300 a month for two bedrooms (2022); she pays literally 10 times more than I do, only because she doesn't own a condo, and lives in the west. What's happening? **To me, it's all about population.** The majority of the American population lives in the East and West regions and the middle is empty. High density drives housing prices higher along with other costs. Here is a question, though: *Do we get paid three times more when we work in East and West?* **Absolutely not.** I think the minimum wages are similar, if not more in the Midwest. Which is why people move to Texas crazily nowadays.

* * *

I was about to graduate from SUNY at Buffalo in March 2006. Most Koreans moved to NYC or its surrounding areas after graduation back then. It is the biggest city in America after all – more importantly, many big Korean communities are there as well. But, at the same time, my girlfriend (wife

74

now) had studied for her doctorate program in Champaign, IL. Simply, I had to choose either going to NYC or Chicago after graduation. By 2006, I had made income out of eBay for about three years. eBay was a bigger venture than Amazon once and I noticed used video games were sold particularly well there. EB games[21] and GameStop were growing popular at that time, too. I thought that I could open a similar business to GameStop, if I can rent a small commercial space. Only difference was that I could sell games on eBay as well, because I had been a power seller since 2003.

After checking some rents in Manhattan one night, I arrived at this conclusion: *There is no way I can go to NYC.* Store rents were like $10,000 a month for 500 sf space in 2006. I truly wondered what kind of business I needed to open to make that much money every month (jewelry?). I ended up having a "900 sf" store space for $1,200 a month in Chicago suburb months later. In a sense, my wife saved me, since *she was the only reason* why I even considered the Midwest. If I chose NYC, my life would have been much different than now (in a miserable way).

I still remember that I saw a GameStop store in Manhattan when I was in NYC for the last time in Feb 2006. Could they charge higher prices for games in Manhattan? **I don't think so.** Every brand new Xbox 360 or PS3 game was $60 everywhere in America, including online, even until I closed my store in 2014. If anyone charges more, players can order it from Amazon, which also charges $60 at most. But did the GameStop in Manhattan pay more rent than my store Cyb Knight? Of course: **They definitely have paid more.** I really have no idea how they could survive.

---

[21] Later, it was purchased by Gamestop.

With the development of IT, people can do a lot of the same jobs everywhere in America now. For example, people can trade stocks online everywhere without working in Wall street. Since traders make or lose the same amount, regardless of locations, *those who live in cheaper locations will make more profit in the end.* Another example could be the writer of the bestseller book *Pachinko*, as I read she is a Korean living in Manhattan. She will make exactly the same amount of royalty whether she lives in a countryside or city. **For sure, she will spend more in Manhattan.** Regardless of regions, I think people tend to spend more, when they live near shopping areas. I see some condos or apartments built right on top of malls. They look fancy, but it's easier for people to find some attractive, but not needed items while walking around.

(Image source: One complex on Roosevelt ave in Chicagoland)

Also, when people live in the middle of nowhere, I think they tend to spend more on gas; it is cheaper to live near some infrastructures, including supermarkets and public transportations.

* * *

Summary

1. Expensive places are often worse places to reside.
2. Buy a house for your own comfort, not just to show it to others.
3. See if you can live in a cheaper State for the same job.

Good job!

You just finished another book!

I am proud of you. And thank you!

Author's Note

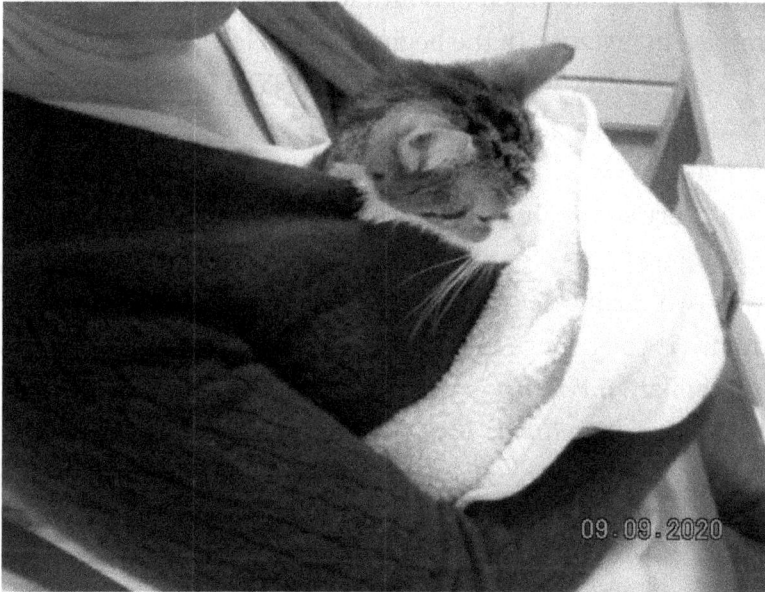

My wife is holding Oscar (2020).

Congratulations: I truly appreciate you finishing my book until the end. The cat in the photo is Yang (Oscar) who I mentioned in *UnBrokable** series; it was taken only a few days before he passed away. We had cherishable memories, but he couldn't get over the blood cancer in the end.

I walked away from my deca-millionaire parents in Korea when I was in my late 20s. Initially, I had lived poorly and worked for diverse jobs in America for over a decade. Eventually, I managed to finish college, get licenses and was able to buy my $60,000 condo in full cash when I became 40. I opened my first stock account and deposited $100 in 2011. Gladly, my portfolio has grown almost to $600,000 by 2024. The *UnBrokable** series shows 80 lessons I have learned along the way.

I was born and raised in South Korea and immigrated to America in my 20s. In the beginning, I failed getting accepted to prestigious Ivy leagues, although SUNY at Buffalo is great. I graduated with a 2.6 GPA by 2005, so I decided not to go to graduate school. Instead, I started my own business, but it wasn't very successful for 8 years. Subsequently, my career at the nursing home also didn't work out as I planned even though I won two certificates during the 7 years; now I try to be an author. If you believe this book can be helpful, ***I would appreciate a rating***. *I do read all the reviews myself and try to learn from them.* I wish my best luck to you!

www.ingramcontent.com/pod-product-compliance
Lightning Source LLC
Chambersburg PA
CBHW070049040426
42331CB00034B/2769